SHORT · S...

RIBBLE

PAUL
HANNON

HILLSIDE PUBLICATIONS
20 Wheathead Crescent
Keighley
West Yorkshire
BD22 6LX

First Published 2010

ISBN 978 1 870141 94 6

The sketch maps are based on 1947 OS one-inch maps and earlier OS six-inch maps

Cover illustration: River Ribble, Stainforth Force
Back cover: Penyghent
Page 1: Ingleborough from Victoria Cave
(Paul Hannon/Hillslides Picture Library)

Printed by Steffprint
Unit 5, Keighley Industrial Park
Royd Ings Avenue
Keighley
West Yorkshire
BD21 4DZ

CONTENTS

INTRODUCTION

Ribblesdale offers some of the finest landscapes in the Yorkshire Dales, with remarkable limestone formations overlooked by sombre mountains. This is the heart of Three Peaks country, and the famous triumvirate of Whernside, Ingleborough and Penyghent are backdrops to many scenes in the district. Along the flanks of these great mountains is an array of gleaming scars and pavements, an unparalleled assembly of gaping potholes and labyrinthine caves, and a network of inviting green trackways over the hills.

Unlike most Dales rivers the Ribble is destined for Lancashire, but from Ribblehead to Hellifield it is proudly one of Yorkshire's finest. This same course is shadowed by the celebrated Settle-Carlisle Railway, a fine monument to Victorian enterprise that is as much a part of the district as the very hills. It is hard now to conceive of its demise, yet only in 1989 was the finest line in England saved from shameful closure. The 72-mile route was completed in 1876 by the Midland Railway, after seven hard years when Victorian endeavour reached new heights to battle against Pennine terrain and weather, and countless viaducts and tunnels were paid for in tragically lost lives.

Settle is a bustling little town that is focal point for an extensive rural area. Tuesday markets present a lively scene when the small square is awash with colour. Facing the square are the historic Shambles, with shops peeping from behind archways, and also a former inn the 'Naked Man', its carved sign of 1633 being a source of some humour. Nearby is The Folly, a large, rambling 17th century house with an intricate façade, and home to the Museum of North Craven Life. Also of note are the Town Hall (1833), Victoria Hall (1853), and Friends' Meeting House (1689).

The majority of walks are on rights of way with no access restrictions. Several also make use of 'Right to Roam' to cross Open Country: these areas can be closed for up to 28 days each year subject to advance notice, though the small sections in these walks are unlikely to be affected. The Countryside Agency and information centres have more details. Many walks can be accessed by bus, with numerous rail stations also to hand. Whilst the route description should be sufficient to guide you around each walk, a map is recommended for greater information: Ordnance Survey 1:25,000 scale maps give the finest detail, and Explorers OL2 and OL41 cover all of the walks.

Langcliffe Scars

USEFUL INFORMATION

·Yorkshire Dales National Park
Colvend, Hebden Road, Grassington, Skipton BD23 5LB
(01756-751600)
·Settle Tourist Information (01729-825192)
·Horton Tourist Information (01729-860333)
·Ingleton Tourist Information (015242-41049)
·Yorkshire Dales Society (01729-825600)
·Open Access (0845-100 3298) www.countrysideaccess.gov.uk
·Traveline - public transport information (0870-6082608)

RIBBLESDALE

20 Short Scenic Walks

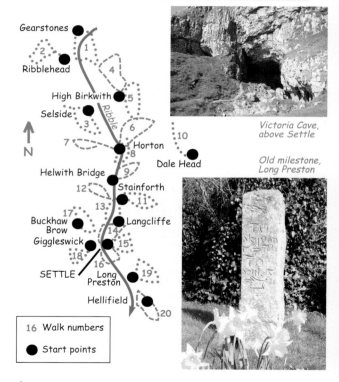

Gearstones
Ribblehead
High Birkwith
Selside
Ribble
N
Horton
Dale Head
Helwith Bridge
Stainforth
Buckhaw Brow
Langcliffe
Giggleswick
SETTLE
Long Preston
Hellifield

Victoria Cave,
above Settle

Old milestone,
Long Preston

| 16 | Walk numbers |
| ● | Start points |

A RECORD OF YOUR WALKS

WALK	DATE	NOTES
1		
2		
3		
4		
5		
6		
7		
8		
9		
10		
11		
12		
13		
14		
15		
16		
17		
18		
19		
20		

4³4 miles
from Gearstones

A beautiful old bridge and ravine are centrepiece of a tramp through wilder upper dale country

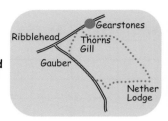

Start Gearstones Lodge (GR: 779799), lay-by to south
Map OS Explorer OL2, Yorkshire Dales South/West

From Gearstones Lodge head south a short way along the road. Ingleborough's classic profile rises beyond Park Fell, with Penyghent further afield to the left. Ignore the first signed path and drop down to find another one just past a barn. From a hand-gate follow the left-hand wall down past barns and over a brow to descend to cross Thorns Gill by way of a delicate packhorse bridge. Thorns Gill is a slender ravine of great charm: the bridge straddles a water-worn gorge, a lovely spot. Note the boulders on pedestals on the opposite bank. Rise half-left, and on the brow head away to the barns amid a cluster of trees at Thorns.

A short enclosed way leads to a junction in front of the main barn, and here go a few strides left to a slim gate on the right into a small enclosure. From the stile opposite head up by the wallside to the brow of Back Hools Hill. This knoll sees Penyghent return beyond the brown, drumlin-strewn moorland. Whernside is behind you, Ingleborough is hidden by Park Fell. Through a gateway drop down a grassy way to a barn. From the stile behind it a soggy path slants across Thorns Moss to a corner gate/stile, passing above a crumbling limekiln. On moorland again a thinner path heads away, bearing gently right and slanting down to cross a meandering little beck. Across, negotiate marshy terrain to rise to a bridle-gate in a fence from where Nether Lodge now appears ahead. A path makes a bee-line for the farming hamlet, slanting gently down to negotiate reedy terrain that is surprisingly less messy.

Joining the drive turn right along it, leading out through rough pasture to a bridge on the Ribble. Beyond this the access road becomes enclosed, winding up past limestone outcrops and doubling back to Ingman Lodge. This fine old farmhouse bears a 1667 datestone above the door. Continue past it and up onto the road. Turn right for a good half-mile as far as the solitary house at Gauber, in a dip on your right. Here take a gate into the yard and cross to successive small gates out into a field. Telegraph poles make a good guide as you drop steadily left to a gate in the wall there. Continue on a faint way down rougher pasture to a gate in the bottom where wall and fence meet. A grassy way heads away, along the base of the minor slope of Goat Close Hill to pass beneath a barn and along to a wooden bridge on a sidestream. Continue on through old walls to rise steadily to a fence-stile by a wooden cabin. Rise left of it to a prominent ladder-stile in the wall above. This puts you back onto the road just south of your starting point.

Packhorse bridge, Thorns Gill

Left: Doorway, Ingman Lodge

*3³⁄₄ miles
from Ribblehead*

**Old farms are linked by
a variety of ways in the
shadow of Whernside
and an iconic rail viaduct**

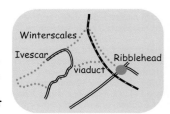

*Start Road junction below pub (GR: 764792), lay-by
Map OS Explorer OL2, Yorkshire Dales South/West*

Ribblehead stands where the road from Ribblesdale meets the Ingleton-Hawes road: only buildings are the Station Inn and some cottages by the railway. The pub has a bunkhouse and one of the finest gents' toilet views in the land. It is the railway that earned national fame for Ribblehead, in the shape of 24-arch Batty Moss Viaduct. This symbol of Victorian enterprise also became the symbol of a hugely successful campaign to prevent cynical closure of the line in the 1980s. All of the Three Peaks are well seen at various stages: mighty Whernside is in view throughout, as your walk is entirely upon its very base. Penyghent is behind you from the outset and will return near the end, while Ingleborough offers its most shapely side for much of the walk.

From the road junction a path heads away to meet a broad track heading for the viaduct from the pub. Just before its arches the track turns to pass beneath them, giving a first glimpse of Ingleborough. Here advance straight on a clear path parallel with the railway. After a brief pull simply remain on the path shadowing the line. Ignoring an early underpass, pass through a gate/stile in a fence and Blea Moor's isolated signal box soon appears ahead. Before reaching it however, a bridleway is met at a second underpass. This time use it, passing beneath the railway and doubling back on this firm track. Ahead is the majestic profile of Ingleborough. The track drops down to join Winterscales Beck to quickly arrive at Winterscales.

Pass through the farming hamlet, crossing a stone-arched bridge to follow the access road out. Over a cattle-grid it emerges at a fork: bear right, maintaining a direct course beneath a wall and later becoming enclosed to run along to the farm at Ivescar. Ignoring another access road branching left, head straight on through the farm with the buildings to your right, and on to a gate at the end. Advance across a field on a fading track beneath a lone house, and a path runs through several fields linked by bridle-gates to approach Broadrake Farm. Here turn left down the drive, and as it turns sharp right and crosses a cattle-grid, leave it by bearing left on a grassy track over rough pasture.

At an early fork go left to a gate/stile. The green track then heads away to ford normally dry Winterscales Beck. If not dry, turn briefly downstream to where it should sink below ground at Gatekirk Sinks. Across, it curves less clearly right to join a surfaced road. Enclosed in trees on the right is the impressive ravine of Gatekirk Cave. Turn left on this farm drive until a fork just after it has bridged the beck: go right to Gunnerfleet Farm. Take the bridge on the right (the lively beck is on the surface here!) and pass along the nearside of the buildings and away along a firm track. Immediately both the viaduct and Penyghent are returned to view. Emerging from a field the track runs on through the open terrain of the common to lead back under the viaduct to finish as you began. Beneath the viaduct a monument celebrates its restoration.

Ribblehead Viaduct

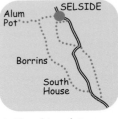

4¹4 miles from Selside

**Quiet paths lead to one of
the Dales' finest cave systems**

*Start North edge of hamlet
(GR: 782757), parking on rough lane
Map OS Explorer OL2,
Yorkshire Dales South/West
Access Alum Pot is on private land: if making detour,
fee payable at Selside Farm in hamlet*

Follow the main road down into the quiet hamlet past Top Farm, with white-walled Selside Farm set back down to the left. Follow the road out: Penyghent's majestic presence will remain throughout. Quickly take a drive up to the right to North Cote. Just past the buildings take a stile on the left and head away to a gate at the far end: Simon Fell rises to the right. With a wall down to your left continue to a stile, with Gill Garth on the skyline ahead. Drop to a kinked wall, only spotting the stile when you're upon it! Across the stream behind climb to a stile by the farm, then curve left over the domed field to find a stile down to the left. This grand viewpoint looks over Selside to a wild Upper Ribblesdale scene dominated by Plover Hill and Penyghent opposite. Drop right from it to a gate then continue this line over an intervening stile, down to a slab crossing of a tiny stream to a gate onto the road.

Go briefly left and cross with care to a stile just short of the drive to Selside Cottages. Double back right in this reedy pasture, diverging from the wall on a faint way to meet a drop to a small stream. A path slants left up the opposite slope, with the railway cottages to the left. Through an old wall advance to a stile ahead, then head off, pathless, across more inviting rough pasture: over to the left is a parallel wall with the railway beyond. Through a gate/stile at the end maintain this line through grassier terrain, rising gently to reach a stile at the far end onto Low Moor. Now bear gently right to drop down to one onto the road.

Double back right, up to a brow and on to a gate/stile on the left. Bear right up past a small scarp, then more gently through scattered limestone and hawthorn to a wall-stile. Cross to another ahead, drop right to one in the wall below, then rise left to a gate into the farm at South House. Pass between the buildings and out on the access road, with further sweeping views. After a cattle-grid it drops right to become enclosed: instead go straight across a sloping pasture to meet another drive in front of the hamlet of Borrins. Don't follow it but take a more inviting track left, joining a wall to cross a stream to a gate. Your invisible path then forks right to follow the wall to a gate/stile. Head away, bearing gently left to a stile ahead: Gill Garth is to your right, with Simon Fell and Park Fell above you. Continue similarly to merge with a wall on your left. This leads to a gate/stile into the head of a green lane. Follow its walled course to a sharp bend: the stony continuation right leads back to the start, but on your left is a stile accessing Alum Pot.

Alum Pot is one of the great names of Yorkshire caving: a broad path rises directly to its tree-shrouded, walled setting. Access is by a stile at the top, though care is needed as the main drop is a sheer 200ft/60m. Above it a thin path slants up to Diccan Pot, above which is Long Churn Pot. Going round by the wall to a stile, Upper Long Churn is found past a pavement before a direct return to Alum. Water from Upper Long Churn travels underground, exposed for the final yards to Diccan: here it runs to enter Alum Pot's shaft. Lower Long Churn interrupts things, with the stream failing to fully surface. Back at the lane, continue along it to finish.

Cavers crossing the moor to Diccan Pot

3 miles from Birkwith

**A remarkable, unexpected ravine
in the heart of bleak moorland**

*Start High Birkwith Farm
(GR: 800768), pay small fee
at farm and park by rough
road to Old Ing, above*
Map OS Explorer OL2, Yorkshire Dales South/West

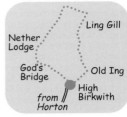

Start by continuing up the stony road past Old Ing to a
gate at the top, where the way forks on meeting the Pennine Way.
From the outset you have big views across to Whernside, Simon
Fell and Park Fell. Turn left on a cart track through a gate, a brief
walled section ending at Calf Holes. Stiles gives access to see a
sizeable moorland beck plunge into a deep limestone hole, caution is
needed! The splendid track then runs a grand level course, with a
wall all the way beneath grassy moorland. With little warning you
reach the massive, wooded ravine of Ling Gill, a true surprise in this
seemingly barren, rolling moorland. With the beck tumbling over
low waterfalls at its heart, the gorge's inaccessibility makes it a
rare example of surviving natural woodland, with ash predominant
amongst limestone favoured trees, and a haven for wildflowers: it
is lined by substantial limestone cliffs. Beyond its head the beck is
crossed at Ling Gill Bridge, the walk's turning point and a place to
linger. A weathered tablet records that this packhorse bridge was
'repaired at the charge of the whole West Rideing - Anno 1765'.

Leaving the Pennine Way to make its climb to Cam Fell,
turn sharp left on a path downstream. It is quickly forced right up
the wallside before the ravine, and fades as you follow the wall
along the edge of rough moorland pasture: Ingleborough and
Whernside are well seen now. Keep above the wall to avoid reeds,
and just past a ruined barn take a stile in the wall. Penyghent makes
a sudden, dramatic appearance here, and remains for most of the
walk. A small trod heads away, with another wall on your left

enclosing a grassy pasture. Towards the bottom a reedier tract is reached: advance to a stile in a fence ahead. Heading away, bear slightly right to meet a fence that points you down to a stile where it meets a sturdy wall. Nether Lodge appears in the bottom, with a lower section of Ling Gill to the left. Continue dropping gently left with the wall through reedy rough pasture. Over an intervening fence-stile the going improves to drop to a moist little depression. Up the other side a short pull onto Swinesett Hill brings better going as the wall leads down to the hamlet of Nether Lodge.

Before the first building take a bridle-gate in the corner on the left, and a footbridge takes you back across Ling Gill Beck. Rise away to a gate on the right, and without passing through join a firm track rising left to ultimately lose itself on a brow. A short restored section takes over, ending abruptly before you drop to a gate at God's Bridge on Brow Gill Beck. This is a classic example of a natural bridge: upstream at Browgill Cave is the resurgence from Calf Holes. A faint path heads away with a wall on your right, rising gently to the start of a track, which quickly passes through a gate/stile. Though one might remain on the track, opt to slant immediately left up the steep grassy slope to cross a brow, where High Birkwith appears below and Old Ing is ahead. Drop to bridge a tiny stream to join the access road linking the two.

Ling Gill Bridge

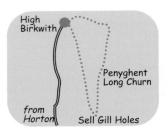

*4½ miles
from Birkwith*

**Old packhorse route and
lush limestone pastures
give easy walking to visit
two splendid potholes**

Start High Birkwith Farm (GR: 800768), pay small fee at
farm and park by rough road to Old Ing, above
Map OS Explorer OL2, Yorkshire Dales South/West

High Birkwith was a packman's inn on the Settle-Hawes
trail. Start by continuing up the stony road past Old Ing to a gate
at the top, where the way forks on meeting the Pennine Way. Turn
right on the main track, ascending through a gate/stile before
easing out. Penyghent appears to the right, with Greenfield Forest
ahead. Take an early fork right to remain on the Pennine Way, a
firm wallside path that curves round to a gate/stile onto reedy
Birkwith Moor. It remains firm to rise left across it, with a sharp
little pull to the summit of the walk. At over 1312ft/400m its
panorama takes in the big cairn on the end of High Greenfield
Knott ahead, and also the 2000+ft mountains of Plover Hill,
Penyghent, Ingleborough, Simon Fell, Whernside and Widdale Fell.

The path drops to meet the old Settle-Langstrothdale
packhorse route at a gate. Pass through and follow it right across
more moorland to a gate. Through this, ford a stream and the track
continues with a wall that remains a constant companion. Through
the next gate you enter lush limestone terrain, with the track now
a super green way. Just short of the next, crumbling wall ahead you
will see a gully just to the left. A detour reveals the pothole of
Penyghent Long Churn. Here the stream plunges underground in a
deep, vertical shaft - be warned! Between this and the wall,
Cowskull Pots is identified by a tree.

Resuming through the gateway, massive Jackdaw Hole is deeply embowered in trees immediately over the wall. Beyond a gate in a wall a fence comes in on the left, and passing through a gateway the track drops down, incorporating an embanked section alongside a small quarry face. While the route now turns right on a grassy way to a ladder-stile alongside a barn, first advance through the gate ahead to Sell Gill Holes. Hard by the path here are an impressive stream entrance and a dry pot. The cavern below is thought to be second only to that of Gaping Gill in magnitude.

Return through the gate and advance to use the ladder-stile. Past the old barn turn right to commence a long, level walk on a broad shelf: easy walking offers big views over Upper Ribblesdale. A faint way through the first two pastures becomes a broad grassy one through an extremely long one. The pasture finally tapers to a gate/stile at the end, hampered by a lively spring: continue to a gate/stile beneath an old limekiln. Through a gate in front the way fades: a slight rise leads to a gate/stile from where a track returns to lead along to a surprisingly deep-cut gill. While there is a stile and footbridge in the bottom, a path takes evasive action by going briefly right to the stream's source beneath rock walls, over a stile and back to the direct line. On approaching a plantation, take a grassy right branch up through rocks to a higher shelf with a blocky escarpment above, then on above the trees to meet a firm track dropping to a gate/stile at the end. Just inside the wooded ravine back to your left is Birkwith Cave, where a stream emerges: a stile gives access. Remain on the wallside track to meet the Old Ing access road.

At Birkwith Cave

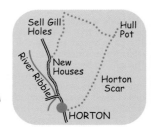

*4½ miles from
Horton-in-Ribblesdale*

**Green lane, moorland and
fieldpath feature in this
visit to a remarkable chasm
in the lap of Penyghent**

Start Village centre (GR: 808726), car park
Map OS Explorer OL2, Yorkshire Dales South/West
Access Open Access, see page 5

For a note on Horton see page 22. From the Penyghent Café cross to a rough lane opposite, and head out of the village. Penyghent rises ahead, with Ingleborough and Whernside rapidly joining in behind. Rising through a gate to an early fork, go left on the walled track of Horton Scar Lane, climbing away before settling down to a long, easy-angled slant. After a short absence Penyghent forms an arresting sight across the deep side valley on your right. The lane improves underfoot and eases further to reach its terminus on the open moor. While the Penyghent ascent path turns right, advance straight on a broad, grassy path for five level minutes to a spectacular arrival at Hull Pot. This magnificent chasm is roughly 300 feet long and 60 feet wide, and it is seen at its best when a waterfall plunges over the northern edge: under normal conditions this will have sunk underground before reaching the hole.

Resume by returning to the gate, but then turn right up a wallside path - the only direction without a sign! On a minor brow it bears away from the wall, down to a dip then climbs to meet a collapsed wall on Whitber Hill. Go right to the wall corner, with Ingleborough and Whernside appearing ahead. Instead of following the broad path down into a quagmire, take a lesser one bearing left. Within 50 yards a thinner trod bears left off it, staying nearer the old wall, and with Horton Quarry appearing ahead drop to a gate in a sturdy wall. Through this continue gently down with an old wall on your left, to pass through a scant wall before a steeper drop. Horton appears, with New Houses directly below. Slant right down this steeper drop to alight onto a broad track, Harber Scar Lane: this is the old Settle-Langstrothdale packhorse route. Just to the right it reaches Sell Gill Holes. Hard by the path are an impressive stream entrance and a dry pot. The cavern below is thought to be second only to that of Gaping Gill in magnitude.

Through the gate leave the main track and quickly bear left on a green way to a stile in the adjacent wall, at an old barn. Double back left on a faint way down the field. Passing through the end of tapering walls, you have a deep dry valley on your left. Continue down, bearing right to a gate in a sturdy wall ahead, then drop right to a corner gateway: the roofs of New Houses are seen ahead. Pass through the old wall behind and bear right to a gate midway along a wall. With New Houses just ahead, drop to a gate in a fence and slant down to the wallside track in the bottom. Go left to enter the rear of a farmyard, and swing right to emerge onto the road. The cosy hamlet of New Houses straddles a cul-de-sac road, and it boasts a surprising number of dwellings. Turn left, over a setted ford and usually superfluous slate clapper bridge, and Horton quickly appears a gentle few minutes' stroll ahead. The Ribble swings in just below to shadow your route back to the village.

Hull Pot in winter

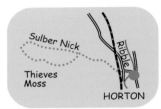

*4¾ miles from
Horton-in-Ribblesdale*

**Remote and popular paths
meet on the limestone
flanks of Ingleborough**

Start Village centre (GR: 808726), car park
Map OS Explorer OL2, Yorkshire Dales South/West
Access Open Access, see page 5

For a note on Horton see page 22. From the Penyghent Café head north into the car park and cross the footbridge at its northern end to by-pass the road bridges by the Crown Hotel. Over the Ribble remain on the roadside footway to a junction at the end. Go straight ahead up a driveway towards the station, taking a small gate to the left onto the platform. Cross the line with care and a little path rises into a field. The path crosses to a small gate just ahead, with the farm at Beecroft Hall appearing. Bear right, the path crossing a large field to the farm drive, with a stile in the wall beyond. It crosses another large field, swinging left further on and up to a gate into a sloping limestone pasture. The path slants up and left across this to run to a gateway in an old wall. It heads away to fork 150 yards further.

Keep straight on the Ingleborough path to pass through a bridle-gate in a wall just ahead, then leave it by rising left alongside the wall: Ingleborough makes its majestic appearance to

20

your right, while ahead is Moughton. Follow it along the short way to where a fence joins it and turn right with the fence. An inviting grass track rapidly forms, close to the fence. After a short while it splits, but remain on the initially more vague left branch to keep faith with the fence. This it successfully does throughout its length, running a splendid course above a limestone escarpment overlooking the plateau of Thieves Moss. Latterly a distant Pendle Hill slots into view. At the far end the errant branch returns for the short stroll to meet the Austwick-Selside bridleway as it comes through a gate in the wall just to the left. Turn right on this for a few minutes' stroll to the Sulber path crossroads.

Here the path ascending Ingleborough from Horton crosses over the Austwick-Selside bridleway. Rejoining the Ingleborough path, turn right on its course through the distinct trough of Sulber Nick. The wayward staggering of Three Peakers is evident in the state of the path after a wet spell. Looking back, Ingleborough quickly returns to view. At the end of the nick it drops down to rejoin the outward route at the bridle-gate from earlier. Pass through, and all that remains is to retrace steps back to Horton, now fully savouring the awesome picture of Penyghent straight ahead.

Left: Horton station   *Penyghent from Sulber*

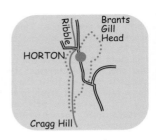

*2¾ miles from
Horton-in-Ribblesdale*

**A steady stroll around the
outskirts of Horton by way
of riverbank, beck, old
lane and a fine ravine**

Start Village centre (GR: 808726), car park
Map OS Explorer OL2, Yorkshire Dales South/West

Horton-in-Ribblesdale is the first village in a valley which
ends in the Irish Sea beyond Preston, and is the centre of Three
Peaks country. It has little intrinsic charm, being a curious mixture
of dwellings strung along the road, and of course overlooked by a
large quarry. Late 17th century datestones adorn several cottage
lintels. Horton's real attraction is its location, as the sight of
boots being pulled on in its over-faced car park will testify: there
is a true walkers' atmosphere here. There is a shop, a campsite and
a renowned cafe that caters for the weary, while pubs are found
at either end. The Crown has two arched bridges outside, while the
Golden Lion faces St Oswald's church: this displays a Norman
doorway, while the solid-looking tower has leanings towards Pisa.

From the Penyghent Café head north through the car
park and cross the footbridge beyond it to by-pass the narrow
road bridges by the Crown. Across the Ribble, take a stile on the
left to follow the river downstream. The Ribble provides company
until reaching a wide, modern footbridge known as the Tay Bridge.
Cross it and double back upstream, quickly passing through a gate.
Penyghent now presents an awesome prospect ahead. Simply follow
the river the short way to a confluence. Here you are deflected
right by the sidestream of Horton Beck, as far as a small footbridge on it. Across, resume on the other bank to reach a driveway
at a large house. Advance along this a short way, and approaching a

cattle-grid before it becomes enclosed, bear left to a ladder-stile in the wall. Cross the small enclosure to a corner wall-stile, and go left, back on the access road. This runs an enclosed course back to the village, re-entering it as suburban Chapel Lane.

Turn right and then sharp left on the side road with the beck on your right. Approaching a farm bear left through the yard and on a short-lived stony, walled track, rising to join a similar track. Ascend briefly right as far as a gate on the left on a minor brow, just before the way dips slightly. Mighty Penyghent ahead is joined by its Three Peaks brethren in the view. Cross the field to a gate ahead and on a longer one to a prominent clump of trees at Brants Gill Head. A stile in the wall to the right of the main trees admits to the vicinity of the beck head. This sizeable resurgence is the beck that sinks at Hunt Pot, high on the flank of Penyghent. In spate it is most spectacular, a series of low falls over rock ledges heralding its return. Contour round above it to a wall-stile at the other side: head away across a sloping field to a gate onto another walled track. This is Harber Scar Lane, which drops down into the village to emerge back alongside the Crown.

Horton Church

23

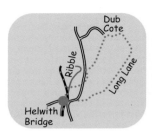

*3¹2 miles
from Helwith Bridge*

**An old green lane leads
to big views and unsung
paths in the very
heart of Ribblesdale**

*Start Hamlet centre (GR: 810694), roadside parking
Map OS Explorer OL2, Yorkshire Dales South/West*

The Helwith Bridge Hotel is a welcoming riverside pub,
while the bridge itself is a dual-purpose structure spanning both
the Ribble and the Settle-Carlisle Railway. It is usually groaning
under the weight of waggons serving quarries that dominate here.
Cross the bridge to a junction, and go left along the main road a
few yards before branching right up Moor Head Lane, a walled
track. When this forks, bear left to commence a long, easy march
up the splendid green way of Long Lane. This section gives ample
time to contemplate the quarries that perhaps represent the
National Park's greatest eyesore. All of the Three Peaks are also
visible, while looking back, Pendle Hill joins a long Bowland skyline.

When the lane finally runs free, your time on it is limited:
while the main route forges on towards Dale Head and Penyghent,
after a few more minutes depart through a gap in the crumbling
wall on your left, and branch off on a level, mercurially surfaced
grassy way. It slants down to a gate, but ignore this in favour of a
gate/stile in the corner just below. Continue down, another grassy
way curving away from the wall to return to it at another gate/stile
combination in the bottom. The descent concludes past Dub Cote,
which has bunkbarn accommodation.

Ignore the main access road going right, and turn left on
another walled access road. When it swings left up to Newlands
House, keep straight on the more inviting green way. Smearsett

Scar rises across the valley, with a Bowland skyline beyond. The way terminates on approaching White Sike Barn. Through the gate take a wall-stile just in front, and drop down to cross the beginnings of a stream before swinging right to a ladder-stile in a wall. Bear left down the large field to a ladder-stile in the descending wall, just above the chirpy stream. Descend the wallside, crossing the stream three further times to reach a ladder-stile in the bottom corner alongside some barns. Turn down the short access track to a gate at New Barn onto the valley road.

Don't join the main road but go left on a curving section of sidelined old road. When it rejoins the road cross and follow the verge left a short way to a wall-stile on your right. Cross the field to a stile at the start of the wall ahead, and follow the wall away until its swings round to the left: here advance straight across the field to a footbridge on the Ribble. Cross and go left on the short enclosed way to pass beneath the railway. Joining an access road, follow this left towards Helwith Bridge. To the left, a low viaduct makes a fine foreground to Penyghent. With the Helwith Bridge Hotel in sight, take a stile to cross a field to emerge onto the road by way of its car park.

Ingleborough and Horton from above Dub Cote

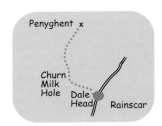

*3 miles
from Rainscar*

**Ribblesdale's own peak is
scaled from a high-level
start: it is still, however,
very much a mountain**

*Start Dale Head (GR: 843714), roadside parking
Map OS Explorer OL2, Yorkshire Dales South/West*

The moorland road from Stainforth to Halton Gill climbs
to a lofty 1420ft/433m crest just a half-mile beyond Dale Head at
Rainscar, and thus affords the shortest route onto Penyghent.
Penyghent is one of the three shapeliest Pennine mountains, along
with Wild Boar Fell and close neighbour Ingleborough. It is the only

member of the Three Peaks to
be crossed by the Pennine Way,
and this walk enjoys an exciting
mile and a half of that famous
route. This is also the only one of
the Three Peaks to attract rock
climbers, thanks to its gritstone
buttresses.

Head along the short
drive to Dale Head Farm: the
dale in question is Silverdale,
which runs south towards
Stainforth. A continuing track
makes its irresistible target
perfectly clear. Through a gate
the way crosses the moor to a
junction at the circular hollow of
Churn Milk Hole. While the

Helwith Bridge-bound track swings left, the ascent path veers right up across the moor to a corner stile abutting the lower section of ridge-wall on Gavel Rigg. From here ascend gently alongside the wall to meet the Horton ascent route at a stile at the foot of Penyghent's south ridge proper, and earn views west to Ingleborough. Without crossing the stile, turn right up the wallside path for the final push, a section comprising two distinct, steeper halves as you tackle first the limestone band, then after a respite, clamber through a boulder-field to engage the upper, gritstone band. Above this you are virtually on the top, and a simple stroll leads up to the OS column, cairn and modern shelter. A sturdy wall runs the full length of the top.

At 2277ft/694m Penyghent's summit is a grand place to be, with extensive views over Three Peaks country and beyond. Dales heights on view include, clockwise, Ingleborough, Simon Fell, Whernside, the Howgill Fells, Baugh Fell, Widdale Fell, Dodd Fell, Great Shunner Fell, Plover Hill, Yockenthwaite Moor, Penhill, Buckden Pike, Great Whernside, Darnbrook Fell, Fountains Fell, Grizedales and Rye Loaf Hill: Pendle Hill and the Bowland moors fill a large area to the south. Until recent times the summit was shown on the map as Penyghent Hill: it can also be seen as Pen-y-Ghent, but in the words of Wainwright that just looks untidy. To leave simply retrace your outward steps, exercising due caution on descending the escarpments.

Left: Penyghent from Dale Head   On Penyghent's south ridge

*3¼ miles
from Stainforth*

**A secretive waterfall is
just the highlight of a
super limestone ramble**

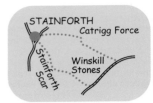

*Start Village centre (GR: 821672), car park
Map OS Explorer OL2, Yorkshire Dales South/West
or Explorer OL41, Forest of Bowland & Ribblesdale*

Stainforth is a sizeable village stood high above and back from the Ribble, and long since by-passed by the road up the dale. Centrally located is the Craven Heifer, a pleasant, multi-roomed pub sporting a popular local name. St Peter's church dates from 1842. A particularly pleasing corner can be found where stepping-stones cross the beck by a small green. Stainforth's best known features, its packhorse bridge and waterfall on the Ribble, are to be found outside the village (see Walk 13). Also on the village edge is the imposing old mansion of Taitlands, a youth hostel for around 60 years until closure in 2007.

Facing the pub, turn a few yards left along the road, then go left along a back lane. As it curves round to the left take a short driveway ahead (to Winskill), with a gate/stile just to the right. Rise up into the field, slanting to a gate ahead and then commencing a greater slant up this extensive pasture, beneath a fence enclosing scrub at the foot of Stainforth Scar. Smearsett Scar is well seen across the valley, with Ingleborough beyond. Stay close to the fence as part way up you use a small gate in it, from where a limestone stepped path climbs concertedly through foliage to reach a ladder-stile out at the top. Views look down the valley to Settle, with Pendle Hill beyond.

Head away on a path above the continuing escarpment to a ladder-stile at the end. Both Whernside and Penyghent have by now appeared to complete the trio. Continue on just a little further then drop left to one in the wall below and cross to Lower Winskill. Head out past the house on the drive which runs to the entrance to Upper Winskill Farm. Turn right on the access road which rises steadily past Winskill Stones to join the Malham Moor road. On a clear day pause here to appraise Lakeland's distant Coniston Fells. Turn left along this unfenced strip of tarmac between limestone outcrops. An old limekiln sits on the right before the brow, which then reveals a fine skyline featuring Penyghent, Plover Hill and Fountains Fell.

Just before dropping to a cattle-grid, double back left down an inviting cart track. This slants down through several fields with Ingleborough dominant ahead. Remain on this all the way down to the bottom corner of a field with a prominent clump of trees behind: this is the location of Catrigg Force. Through the gate is the head of Goat Scar Lane. Before heading down it, first savour the waterfall detour. Through a small gate on the right a short path drops down to the top of the waterfall, where with great care you

can peer down to the bottom. The conventional view can be sampled by entering the trees on the left to descend a good path to the foot of the ravine. This is as lovely as any waterfall in the Dales. Returning to Goat Scar Lane, turn down its stony, enclosed course all the way into Stainforth, emerging onto a green.

Catrigg Force

*3³⁄₄ miles
from Stainforth*

**A gentle ascent to a
stunning viewpoint, with
much interest en route**

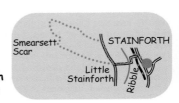

*Start Village centre (GR: 821672), car park
Map OS Explorer OL2, Yorkshire Dales South/West
Explorer OL41, Forest of Bowland & Ribblesdale
Access Open Access, see page 5*

From the car park turn right on the main road, leaving almost immediately by a road left. Bridging the railway it descends to cross 17th century Stainforth Bridge, built to serve the York-Lancaster packhorse trade. Continue up to a junction at Little Stainforth, a hamlet also known as Knight Stainforth: its three-storey hall dates largely from the 17th century. Head up the farm drive opposite, continuing up the enclosed track to a stile at the top. A good track rises away, fading in a vast, sloping pasture. Head directly up the centre, and on the brow, if not before, pause to enjoy a big Ribblesdale prospect. Smearsett Scar appears ahead as you advance to a gate/stile. Continuing to a gentle brow, its profile extends to Pot Scar, enclosing their hidden valley. The path slants left down to a stile in the wall just short of the corner. Though it runs invitingly on through this upland trough, advance only to the wall corner on your right, then turn right on a wallside path to a stile in a kink directly beneath the crest of Smearsett Scar. A thin path ascends the wallside to its brow, from where strike left up through the edge of the outcrops to quickly attain the summit.

At 1191ft/363m Smearsett Scar has an OS column, a pile of stones and three shelters: its south face falls away sharply, with low crags giving way to scree slopes. This is probably the finest spot for appraising the Ribblesdale landscape. Included are Horton and Helwith Bridge backed by Plover Hill, Penyghent and

Fountains Fell: then come Stainforth, its Scar, and then Settle's inimitable hills. To the south is a distant Pendle Hill, and northwards a tip of Whernside peeps around Ingleborough presiding over its limestone entourage. Pot Scar looks enticing further west along the undulating escarpment.

Leave by heading west on a thin trod along the edge, bound towards Pot Scar, its gleaming limestone a favourite haunt of climbers. Part way on, however, a scarp deflects you 'inland', and here continue slanting right down the pasture to a crumbling wall, dropping to a sturdy one with a slight rise to meet the Feizor Nick-Little Stainforth path. Don't pass through the gate/stile but turn right, a very gentle rise to a brow where Ingleborough disappears. This delectable green way continues, dropping gently towards the Ribblesdale scene, with Stainforth appearing. Approaching a wall it forks: take the right branch to a ladder-stile. By now majestic Penyghent has joined Fountains Fell to the left. Drop slightly right to a ladder-stile in the bottom, and from one just beneath it drop down the wallside of a large field. From the gate/stile at the end a track drops down to a gate onto a back road, but the right of way drops sharply left to a gate in front of tree-sheltered Hargreaves Barn, and an enclosed grassy way runs down onto the road at the same point. Turn right to Little Stainforth, and finish as you began. At Stainforth Bridge you can now take time to enjoy the delights of Stainforth Force, downstream, before returning to the village.

Pot Scar and Ingleborough from Smearsett Scar

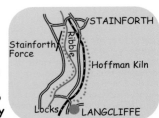

*3³⁴ miles
from Langcliffe*

**Two villages linked with a
feast of interest, from
riverbank and waterfall to
ancient bridge and industry**

*Start Village centre (GR: 822650), car park at old school
Map OS Explorer OL2, Yorkshire Dales South/West
or Explorer OL41, Forest of Bowland & Ribblesdale*

Langcliffe is a lovely village with a spacious green. By the
phone box a tablet on a house depicts the Naked Woman, modestly
dated 1660 and once an inn. Leave by a rough lane to the left of the
old school: quickly reaching a junction bear right on a walled track
out of the village. Within minutes two paths go off left: take the
first leaving a small gate to run an enclosed fieldside course down
onto a track. Go briefly left to the valley road and turn right over
the parallel footbridge over the railway. Across the road, descend
a short-lived lane to old millworkers' cottages at Locks: you meet
the Ribble where an attractive scene incorporates a weir.
        Cross the footbridge and turn upstream. At the end of a
long pasture after an old paper mill you are parted from the Ribble,
passing a lively spring, but that aside, its bank leads unerringly to
Stainforth Bridge. Just beyond the confluence where Stainforth
Beck enters, you reach the delights of Stainforth Force. Bridge,
riverbank, waterfall and adjacent caravan site combine to make
this a place of popular resort: the idyllically sited falls are a rare
burst of activity for the Ribble. Just beyond the falls you join a
narrow back road at the graceful 17th century Stainforth Bridge,
built to serve the York-Lancaster packhorse trade. Cross and
ascend the steeply climbing lane, which bridges the railway to join
the valley road. Go right then left into Stainforth.

Continue past the Craven Heifer pub south along the street to rejoin the main road. A short way along the footway take a stile on the left and head along the field to a gate/stile. Cloaked in trees up to the left is Stainforth Scar. Continue towards the end of the next field where a fence-stile puts you into the environs of the old Craven Lime Works. An informative trail has been devised, and a short choice awaits. Either go left for the old winding house and then down an incline, or right for the massive triple draw kilns of 1872. The paths rejoin beyond them to run to a wall-stile across a slab bridge, revealing the amazing Hoffman Kiln in front. On your left is a tunnel entrance through which horse-drawn waggons brought blocks of limestone out of the quarry above: constructed in 1873, the kiln features 22 individual chambers, and working round the clock it occupied no less than 90 workers at its peak!

At the far end drop into a car park. Pass left of a house and follow the access road out, passing a car park and a red-brick weigh-house. Just after this a short path detours left up to the remains of the Spencer Kilns. Just further the road swings right to pass under the railway to the valley road. Don't follow it but take an enclosed cart track on the near side of the line. Through a gate/stile at the end it emerges into a field. Undulating along towards the far side, as it turns uphill keep straight on to a stile ahead. A thinner path takes over, crossing to a stile on a gentle brow: look back to appraise a fine prospect up the valley. Continue to a stile ahead, then bear left across to a corner stile onto the grassy lane at the start. Turn right to finish as you began.

At the Hoffman Kiln

*3¹2 miles
from Settle*

**A lovely village sits amid
a host of absorbing
features either side of
the Ribble above Settle**

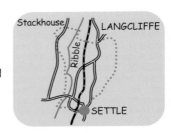

Start Town centre (GR: 819636), car parks
Map OS Explorer OL2, Yorkshire Dales South/West
or Explorer OL41, Forest of Bowland & Ribblesdale

From the Town Hall by the market place cross the main road and head down Kirkgate, passing the Friends' Meeting House of 1689. Under the railway bridge keep straight on, passing a supermarket on the left. At the bend leave the road and go on a footway left of the fire station. At the end swing right to pass around the back of the historic Kings Mill, a recent conversion to residential use. Go left to a footbridge over the Ribble and turn upstream on a footway to the main road bridge.

Cross the road and head straight off along an enclosed path between sports fields: ahead, Penyghent looks magnificent. At the end join the river briefly before being ushered away into a field. Cross to a prominent stile to enjoy a good section above a steep wooded riverbank: directly below is Langcliffe paper mill. Emerging again, this time bear left to a stile onto Stackhouse Lane. Turn right to reach the edge of Stackhouse. This cosy grouping of exclusive dwellings huddles beneath the hill and is clearly happy to remain hidden in its protective greenery. A short loop gives a slightly closer look: take the first rough road into it, turning first right along what becomes a grassy cart track, then right again back onto the road. Just a few yards further, take a walled green path to the right to meet the Ribble at Locks, an attractive scene that incorporates a weir.

Across the footbridge turn right along a street between old millworkers' cottages. At the end a snicket runs left to an old millpond. Turn right on the path running along the length of this hugely attractive large pond. At the end the path swings left between pond and mill to drop onto an access road. Go left to the junction ahead alongside a caravan park, then go straight ahead on a walled snicket. This rises to bridge the railway and up onto the valley road at Langcliffe. Cross to a side road virtually opposite and head along into the village centre. By the phone box look for a tablet on a house wall depicting the Naked Woman, modestly dated 1660: once an inn, it was a close friend of Settle's more famous Naked Man.

Emerging onto the spacious green, remain on the road past the fountain and along between the old school on the left and the church, right. As the road leaves the village by passing through a gateway prior to climbing away, instead take a gate to the right. A steep path ascends past a spring to a gate at the top. Bear right on a thin, lower path above a wall. Levelling out it gives a bird's-eye picture of Langcliffe with Ingleborough beyond, while up-dale, Penyghent overtops Stainforth Scar. At a bridle-gate advance on to a gate/stile in another wall to merge with a bridleway from the left. On again, becoming briefly enclosed, Settle is laid out as on a map. Following a wall to a gate at the end, a restored path makes an enclosed descent of Banks Lane onto a back lane at the top of Constitution Hill. Turn left to drop down into the market place.

The Ribble at Locks

*4 miles
from Settle*

**An enthralling exploration
of the limestone heights
overlooking Settle**

Start **Town centre (GR: 819636), car parks**
Map **OS Explorer OL2, Yorkshire Dales South/West
or Explorer OL41, Forest of Bowland & Ribblesdale**

Leave the market place by Constitution Hill, left of the Shambles. After a steep pull the road turns left, almost at once abandon it in favour of the rougher Banks Lane to the right. This restored path resumes the climb between walls to emerge into open country. Already there are big views back over Settle and Giggleswick and across to the Bowland moors, while Ingleborough appears before the lane ends. At once the way forks: take the right branch slanting up the bank, passing through an old wall then quickly turning to ascend more directly. Merging with a wall from the left it rises to a gate at the top. Keep on, the early fork giving alternative options on broad grassy paths that will shortly merge again. Now level, ahead is the magnificent scenery of Warrendale Knotts and Attermire Scar. The path drops down into this upland bowl, over a stile and along to a gateway below Attermire Scar. Attermire Cave is a dark slit located high up the limestone cliff. For those agile enough to reach its entrance, it can be penetrated a fair way with a sense of adventure and a reliable torch. Just prior to the gateway are the remnants of an old shooting range.

Through the gateway take the wallside path rising left to a nick, then on through a trough on a fine green way: Ingleborough and Whernside fill the open view ahead. A wall joins you to rise to a kissing-gate ahead, and a thinner path resumes alongside the wall beneath scree at the foot of a limestone scar.

The entrance to Victoria Cave can be gleaned by the wall of clean rock above it, and a thin path detours up to it. Before approaching it consider the warnings of the perils of rockfalls. The massive entrance has been blasted to this size in modern times, but the cave's history goes back through countless periods. It has yielded evidence of a richly varied occupancy, including bones of rhinoceros, hippopotamus, bear, mammoth and Stone Age man. Another path slants back down to the main one to resume, quickly reaching a kissing-gate onto the unsurfaced Gorbeck Road.

Turn left through the gate and descend the track to join the steep road climbing out of Langcliffe. At once, however, take a bridle-gate on the left and head away on a splendid path, passing beneath a wood and above a steep fall to Langcliffe and the valley. Behind you is a fine prospect of Penyghent. Two further bridle-gates are met before the path curves down a big sloping pasture to a bridle-gate at the end. Through this follow a wall away to merge with a lower bridleway a little further. Simply remain on this, briefly enclosed, then on to merge with the outward route to descend Banks Lane back down into town.

At Warrendale Knotts

*4 miles
from Settle*

**Riverbank, old tracks and
massive views on the lesser
known side of Settle**

Start Town centre
(GR: 819636), car parks
Map OS Explorer OL2, Yorkshire Dales South/West
or Explorer OL41, Forest of Bowland & Ribblesdale

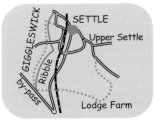

From the Town Hall by the market place cross the main
road and head on Kirkgate, passing the old Friends' Meeting House.
Under the railway bridge keep straight on past a Georgian house on
the right and a supermarket left. At the bend leave the road for a
footway left of the fire station. At the end swing right to pass
round the back of historic Kings Mill, a conversion to residential
use. Go left to a footbridge on the Ribble and turn downstream. The
modern path soon ends at a gate/stile, and a more traditional path
resumes down the grassy bank. Before long a stile takes you into an
enclosed path alongside sports fields on the edge of Giggleswick.
At the end pass through a wall-gap into housing. Bear left then left
again as the road swings right, and a path runs between gardens out
onto a road. Leaving suburbia, cross to a stile opposite and a thin
path crosses the field to regain the river at a gate/stile. Head
downstream on a lovely stretch of open bank, through further
stiles to ultimately become confined by the by-pass to your right.

After an enclosed spell the river swings right under the
by-pass. Don't look for a footbridge but take a stile on your right
to ascend to the by-pass, and use its footway to cross the river. At
the other end escape back down the bank to a bridle-gate onto the
riverbank. Joining a stony track go briefly right then forsake the
river as the track becomes enclosed to head away, absorbing Runley
Mill's drive to rise to the old road. A milestone is inscribed with
hands to Settle, Skipton and Clitheroe: an old tollhouse stands on

the road opposite. Cross over and up a rough access road. This drive to Lodge Farm begins a sustained pull, initially over the railway then more firmly uphill all the way to the farm, with its imposing house of 1875. During this time big views open out back over the valley, with Penyghent over the town and then Ingleborough dominant.

From a gate at the top turn left along the enclosed track, over a stream and swinging right to a fork. Take the right option to resume the climb, as a super old way rising through a gate/stile and by attractive woodland. Higher, it levels out, with colourful Peart Crags on your left. It now rises only gently, swinging left through further colourful surrounds to reach a gate, the summit of your walk at last. Though a stony track leads onto an old road, you take a stile on the left. A good path heads away with a wall on your right through moor-grass, improving further to drop to a stile just short of the corner. Superb views look over the town with its steep limestone hills on your right, to a landscape overseen by mighty Ingleborough.

A thin path heads away, dropping more steeply at the end to a gate/stile overlooking a steep drop. A thin path turns right to slant down the wallside, near the end passing through a gate for a few enclosed yards to another, then along a wallside to a gate onto Mitchell Lane. Turn left to the fringe of Upper Settle, meeting a through road at a little green by Chapel House. Go left down here through characterful corners to emerge by The Folly, a rambling 17th century house with an intricate façade: it incorporates the Museum of North Craven Life. The centre is just a minute further.

Descending back to Settle

3½ miles
from Buckhaw Brow

Easy walking around a
wide range of limestone
features overlooking
Buckhaw Brow

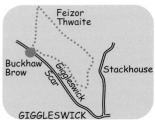

Start Lay-by (GR: 797657),
on east side of summit at top of climb from Settle
Map OS Explorer OL41, Forest of Bowland & Ribblesdale

Buckhaw Brow is a road climb that was an animated scene prior to Settle by-pass opening. From the lay-by a gate sends a path slanting left up through a cleft in the limestone atop Giggleswick Scar. Almost from the outset Pendle Hill and Bowland's moors rise across the Ribble Valley. Things quickly level out to fork just short of a hand-gate in the adjacent wall. You shall return through that, but for now fork sharp right on a thinner path parallel with an old wall to your right. On through a small limestone pavement the way runs beneath limestone scars but high above the wooded main scar. Over a stile in a sturdy wall the path runs on through increasingly enchanting surroundings. Caves over to the left include Kinsey Cave, which has yielded evidence of occupation by long extinct animals.

A little further a minor brow reveals Schoolboys Tower ahead. The path drops gently past a prominent cairn on a mound: a detour past it sends a trod 150 yards down to the tower, a large cairn erected by Giggleswick School pupils. Beneath is the rim of a massive quarry. Double back left, a path forming to rejoin the main one which runs well outside the quarry fence, passing a cairned knoll to reach a crumbling wall: Penyghent and Fountains Fell enter the scene. At this corner turn sharp right between old wall and quarry fence, to descend with an appreciation of the quarry's scale.

When wall and fence diverge abandon the quarry to follow a broad green way near the wall. Towards the bottom of this big bowl double back left on a similar green way through the old wall. It crosses a large, sloping rough pasture, rising slightly to ascend through scattered trees. Penyghent enjoys a game of 'cat and mouse' as it comes and goes from view. When a left branch curves uphill, advance straight on to a wall corner just ahead. Follow the wall-top away until a stile admits to the wood. The path runs to the edge of the trees then falters. Cross to the left-hand of two stiles in the wall ahead, and a path rises away to merge with one from the other stile. Follow it up through the left-hand of two gateways, from where it winds more steeply up, briefly. On levelling out it forks, though merges a short way further, above a wall corner to head on through a gate. The track remains close by the right-hand wall to a gate at the far end: enjoy a brief glimpse of Ingleborough.

   Through the gate is another path junction: bear left to a gate in the wall corner just ahead and head off on a green track. Beyond another gate this soon rises with a wall to bring Ingleborough into the scene. As the wall parts company continue to the next gate. The cluster of Austwick appears ahead: to your right is Pot Scar. As the track gently descends to a guidepost, take a path doubling sharply back left. It angles towards the nearby wall, and along to a corner gate/stile. Head away with the wall, which quickly turns off to let your broad green way strike across the field centre to a gate/stile. It continues to a small gate in the wall ahead: head away to drop through a minor scarp to the small gate from five minutes into the walk, taking the right branch to drop back to the road.

Giggleswick Scar

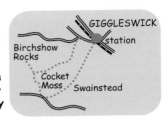

*4½ miles
from Giggleswick*

**Delightful walking through
a landscape seemingly far
from typical Dales scenery**

*Start Railway station (GR: 803628),
car park here and lay-by back along road*
Map OS Explorer OL41, Forest of Bowland & Ribblesdale

The railway at Giggleswick is paralleled by the by-pass, with the Craven Arms directly opposite: Giggleswick village is a mile distant. From the station use steps down to the by-pass, and take a side road under the railway. Passing Swaw Beck Farm it rises to a junction: take the narrower left branch, and in 100 yards go left up a rough, walled lane. Look back to the start of near permanent views over the Ribble to Settle's limestone hills, backed by Rye Loaf Hill and Fountains Fell. The lane runs in a field: look back to find Penyghent entering the scene above Giggleswick Quarry, while further left Ingleborough's classic outline appears. Also prominent is the dome of Giggleswick School chapel. Cross to the far corner where a stile leads to a gate onto a green way, Cocket Lane. Turn up its partly restored course, which accommodates a small stream: Rome Crag is well seen to the right. Emerging into a broadening, rough pasture at the end, rise by the left-hand wall to a brow.

As the wall turns away, Cocket Moss appears below. Bear left above its fence and drop to a gate in the corner beneath Moor Close Crag. A solid, embanked track bridges the mire to a bouldery brow behind. Continue to a minor brow just short of a wall. While your onward route is left, detour right for a look at Birchshow Rocks. Excellent turf leads to a gate at the end, with the distinctive rocks ahead. Head away with the wall, and as it ends advance to a suitable point beneath the rocks to appraise this splendid array.

Back on the edge of Cocket Moss, keep straight on the wallside past your arrival point and down through damp terrain to a corner stile. Head away to merge with the wall on the right, over an intervening stile then on a long, rough pasture by the right-hand wall. A few boulders are passed and moist moments encountered. As the wall drops away keep straight on, through gates in intervening fences to drop to a corner stile onto a back road. At once turn left along an enclosed track, Swainstead Raike. At the end it emerges into a no-man's-land, meeting a track just ahead. Bear briefly right on it, then cut back left to a gate above the highest trees lining the tiny stream. A green rake bears right above the beck, then a pathless way runs atop the wooded bank in this stony pasture of Coney Garth. Towards the bottom bear a little left to a wall-stile into a pocket oakwood. Bear left out of it to contour on to a fence-stile, then cross a large, sloping field to approach Littlebank.

Littlebank's drive is joined but not followed, as a stile admits to the outer garden: descend to a kissing-gate in the far corner. Drop left down the field to a stile where wall and fence meet. Cross to a wall-stile in front of the farm at Littlebank Barn, and across a small enclosure between barns and house, head directly away with a wall on your left. Through a gate at the end bear slightly left to a wall-stile, then advance over a low brow with the wall, taking a stile near the end to cross a field corner to the next. Cross to another into the last field, with the station ahead. A stile at the far corner leads to the road under the railway bridge to finish.

Birchshow Rocks

43

*4¾ miles
from Long Preston*

**Unassuming but delightful
paths access an old
green lane in a quiet
corner of the Dales**

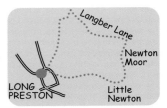

Start Village green (GR: 834582), roadside parking
Map OS Explorer OL2, Yorkshire Dales South/West
or Explorer OL41, Forest of Bowland & Ribblesdale

Long Preston is a pleasant village whose focal point is the green, graced by a maypole. Facing it is the Maypole Inn, with the Boars Head and a Post office/store/tearoom nearby. From the back of the green head along School Lane. Just past a junction behind the school a walled grassy path heads off left. This cuts a corner of the road, but omits the church. For this, remain on the narrow lane. The church gate is to the right, around a corner. St Mary's has a low-slung roof and a Norman font with Jacobean cover.

Leave along the church front to a little gate out of the yard back onto New House Lane. Already you have views over the Ribble Valley to the landmark of Pendle Hill: it will remain in sight for most of the walk. Picking up the direct route, continue on the downgrading lane. At a fork ignore the right one which drops to some sheds, while the left one leads on through more open terrain before rising to Little Newton. Keep left of the farm buildings to pens at the end, then from a gate on the left join the bank of Newton Gill. Within yards a shapely bridge carries you over it and a grass track accompanies it upstream. It fades at Waterfall Rock, where exposed tilted rock strata overlook a hollow above a minor waterfall. Just beyond, a stile admits to a corner of Newton Moor.

Resuming upstream a little path drops to shadow the beck, while a higher trod runs on from above the stile. As the slopes open out rise a little on a faint trod over rough moor-grass. Curve round level ground above a confluence and wall corner, with the beck and parallel wall to the left, to reach a junction with the next wall ahead. Down to the left a stile and bridge are not seen until upon them. Go briefly left up the wallside to a stile on the brow, then slant right up a vast reedy pasture to approach a wall-corner on the left. Ahead, a ladder-stile onto Langber Lane beckons. Turn left on this old green way, becoming firmer surfaced at Bookilber Barn. Ingleborough is briefly revealed ahead, while to the left are the South Pennines, Pendle Hill, the West Pennine Moors, Waddington Fell and Bowland.

Leave when the track winds down above Bookil Gill Beck on the left. Doubling sharply back, ignore a ladder-stile to pass through a gate. A few yards downstream ford the beck, and a green path heads away. As the beck swings more steeply left, the path contours around through an old wall. Head straight on past a couple of trees on the brow to descend through successive gates, down a spur above a confluence. Through a kissing-gate cross to a foot-bridge on Long Preston Beck, and join a track slanting up the bank to the top of New Pasture Plantation. Look back up this side valley to glimpse limestone tors above Settle. Just yards beyond an access stile take another stile to forsake the now walled New Pasture Lane. Aim directly away from the corner, on the brow locating a stile ahead. Descend right to another stile, and further obvious stiles lead you on. Diagonally across a couple more fields to a stile beyond a pool, two final fields are crossed to find a corner-stile onto Green Gate Lane. Go left to finish.

Long Preston church

45

*3¾ miles
from Hellifield*

**A gentle ramble links two
historic buildings where the
Ribble leaves the Dales**

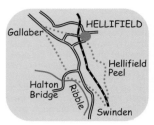

*Start Village centre
(GR: 855564), car park*
Map OS Explorer OL41, Forest of Bowland & Ribblesdale

Hellifield is Yorkshire's last village on the Ribble. Its railway station with café stands where the Leeds-Settle-Carlisle/ Morecambe line is joined by a branch from Lancashire. It has a Post office, shops, chippy, the Black Horse pub and St Aidan's church. From the car park don't join the main road but head south on the street past a former chapel to the village edge: when the road turns sharp right advance straight on an access road at The Green. This runs through parkland to Hellifield Peel, an imposing house with a long and colourful history, much of it in the hands of the Hamertons. After holding World War Two prisoners it fell into ruin, but has enjoyed an award-winning 21st century restoration.

Don't enter but take a track left of the grounds to a gate just past them. Through it ignore the track climbing the field, and go right with the ha-ha before crossing the field centre to a stile at the far side. Advance on to a gate ahead, where a track leads on to merge with the rail embankment. At the end it passes under the line and bears left to Swinden. At the first barn your way takes a track doubling back right after a five-minute detour: to the right of the farmyard a wall-stile in a recess admits to the drive, and a few yards further you can appraise splendid Swinden Hall. It has a three-storey porch with a 1657 lintel, and some intriguing windows.

Back at the stile take the track dropping to Mansell Beck. Across, take the track through the right-hand gate, rising to a brow where it ends at a gate in the adjacent fence. Pass through and follow the fence right, through an intervening gate and on to a stile at the end. This modest brow reveals the Peel across to the right and the hills behind Hellifield ahead. Head away with a broad sunken way: on a brow the pasture narrows and the A682 appears below. Drop left to a stile onto it, crossing to a wooded bank. A path slants down to emerge onto the bank of the Ribble. Turn upstream to Halton Bridge, and a kissing-gate puts you onto a road.

Go briefly right then turn left on a drive to a ramshackle cluster of buildings at Pan Beck Farm. Across the bridge go right to a gate into a field, and cross to follow the base of a wooded bank away. When the trees end continue with a fence to a stile at the far corner. Now you trace a fence along a modest bank top with views to Hellifield and Settle's limestone hills. At a narrowing above sewage works the fence turns left: advance straight on the field centre, finding a gate by sheep pens in the far corner back onto the A682. Go cautiously left a short way, passing an old milestone (Settle 5, Gisburn 6) hidden under the hedge. At a narrow lane escape right.

Through a gate by a bungalow bear off right, an enclosed path emerging to reach a drive serving the modern development on your right. Cross a lawn and another drive to a path dropping to a stile and plank bridge. Head away with trees and stream to your left, passing its resurgence to a gate ahead. Follow the wall away to a brow where it turns off, and keep straight on past Beck House to a wall-stile in the corner beyond. Maintain this line to a fence-stile and a footbridge on Hellifield Beck, beyond which a wall-stile puts you onto a narrow road. Turn left under the railway to finish.

Hellifield Peel

HILLSIDE GUIDES... cover much of Northern England

Other colour *Pocket Walks* guides (more in preparation)

·UPPER WHARFEDALE   ·LOWER WHARFEDALE
·UPPER WENSLEYDALE   ·LOWER WENSLEYDALE
·MALHAMDALE   ·SWALEDALE   ·RIBBLESDALE
·INGLETON/WESTERN DALES   ·SEDBERGH/DENTDALE
·NIDDERDALE   ·HARROGATE/KNARESBOROUGH
·BOWLAND   ·AROUND PENDLE   ·RIBBLE VALLEY
·AMBLESIDE/LANGDALE   ·BORROWDALE
·AIRE VALLEY   ·ILKLEY/WASHBURN VALLEY

Our *Walking Country* range features more great walks...

· WHARFEDALE   ·MALHAMDALE   ·WENSLEYDALE
·HARROGATE & the WHARFE VALLEY   ·SWALEDALE
·RIPON & LOWER WENSLEYDALE   ·NIDDERDALE
·THREE PEAKS ·HOWGILL FELLS · HOWARDIAN HILLS
·TEESDALE   ·EDEN VALLEY   ·ALSTON & ALLENDALE

·ILKLEY MOOR   ·BRONTE COUNTRY   ·CALDERDALE
·PENDLE & the RIBBLE   ·WEST PENNINE MOORS
·ARNSIDE & SILVERDALE   ·LUNESDALE   ·BOWLAND

·LAKELAND FELLS, SOUTH   ·LAKELAND FELLS, EAST
·LAKELAND FELLS, NORTH   ·LAKELAND FELLS, WEST

Long Distance Walks
·COAST TO COAST WALK ·CUMBRIA WAY ·DALES WAY
·LADY ANNE'S WAY   ·NIDDERDALE WAY
·WESTMORLAND WAY   ·FURNESS WAY
·PENDLE WAY   ·BRONTE WAY   ·CALDERDALE WAY

Visit www.hillsidepublications.co.uk
or write for a catalogue